THE ULTIMATE
UNAUTHORIZED
STAR TREK
QUIZ BOOK

THE ULTIMATE
STAR TREK

UNAUTHORIZED
QUIZ BOOK

ROBERT W. BLY

HarperPerennial
A Division of HarperCollins*Publishers*

THE ULTIMATE UNAUTHORIZED STAR TREK QUIZ BOOK. Copyright © 1994 by Robert W. Bly. All rights reserved. Printed in the United States of America. No part of this book may be used or reproduced in any manner whatsoever without written permission except in the case of brief quotations embodied in critical articles and reviews. For information address HarperCollins Publishers, Inc., 10 East 53rd Street, New York, NY 10022.

HarperCollins books may be purchased for educational, business, or sales promotional use. For information, please write: Special Markets Department, HarperCollins Publishers, Inc., 10 East 53rd Street, New York, NY 10022.

FIRST EDITION

ISBN 0-06-273321-4

94 95 96 97 98 ◆/RRD 10 9 8 7 6 5 4 3 2 1

To Bonita Nelson—agent and friend

CONTENTS

ACKNOWLEDGMENTS

I'd like to thank Bonita Nelson, my agent, for having faith in me and enthusiasm for the book. Thanks also to Rob Kaplan, for sharing our enthusiasm and for being far more patient than I deserve.

Thanks also to my wife Amy, and sons Alex and Stephen, for putting up with the long hours that preparing this book necessitated.

INTRODUCTION

Who was NBC's first choice for the role of Captain Kirk?

What is the serial number of the U.S.S. Enterprise?

Exactly how fast is warp factor 3?

What space station becomes overrun with tribbles?

Star Trek is much more than a TV show that ran for less than three full seasons: it's a national mania. Every year, "Trekkers" (*Star Trek* fans) spend millions of dollars to buy *Star Trek* collectibles, read *Star Trek* books, go to *Star Trek* conventions and watch *Star Trek* movies. No other television show has ever had such a following.

Get two or more Trekkers in a room, and they'll soon be challenging each other's knowledge of *Star Trek* legend and lore. ("What is the life span of the average Vulcan?" "What actor was originally approached for the role of Spock?" "Who are Worf's adoptive earth parents?")

For you and thousands of other *Star Trek* fans, *The Ultimate Star Trek Quiz Book* has been written. It is the one trivia book designed to test the knowledge of every fan, from the casual *Star Trek* watcher to the convention-attending enthusiast. The book spans the whole spectrum of *Star Trek*, from the original TV show, books and movies to *Star Trek: The Next Generation* and *Deep Space Nine*. Those who like to catch an occasional rerun now and then will enjoy learning "behind the scenes" details of *Star Trek*, while serious *Star Trek* buffs will discover some little-known but fascinating facts.

The original mission of the U.S.S. Enterprise was a five-year voyage, but *Star Trek* has gone way beyond that. The first six *Star Trek* movies, for example, have grossed more than $474 million in box office revenues, while *Star Trek: The Next Generation* has, at times, been the highest-rated weekly syndicated TV series in America.

More than 100 *Star Trek* novels have been published and, according to *TV Guide* magazine, there are over 500 amateur and professional *Star Trek* fan publications. Sales of *Star Trek* merchandise are approximately one-half billion dollars.

I hope you enjoy *The Ultimate Star Trek Quiz Book*. If you think you've found an error, please write and let me know. And if you have a favorite *Star Trek* fact that isn't included, please send it along so I can share it with readers of the next edition of this book. Please write:

BOB BLY
22 E. Quackenbush Avenue
Dumont, NJ 07628

➤ *Early Starts*

1) What studio first asked Gene Roddenberry to do *Star Trek*?

2) What was the name of the ship's original captain?

3) Mr. Spock was originally half human and half this.

4) What was Spock's original rank?

5) This person, not Sulu, was the original ship's navigator.

6) He, not Dr. McCoy, was the first ship's doctor and nicknamed "Bones."

7) Name the woman who was second in command to the captain before Spock assumed that position.

8) What was the original name of the *Star Trek* space cruiser, before Enterprise?

9) In what part of outer space was this ship to conduct its mission?

10) When MGM rejected the original concept for *Star Trek*, who took it?

➤ *First Pilot Episode*

1) What was the title of the first pilot for *Star Trek*?

2) Name the two cast members from the first pilot who became regulars in the *Star Trek* TV series.

3) Who played the ship's captain in the original pilot?

4) What planet did the action take place on?

5) Why did the inhabitants of this planet live below the surface?

6) How much did it cost to make this pilot episode?

7) When was the first pilot originally aired?

8) Why did the aliens kidnap the Enterprise's captain?

9) Name the Earth spaceship that had crash-landed on the planet 20 years before.

10) How did the captives finally return to the planet's surface?

➤ *Second Pilot Episode*

1) What was the title of the second pilot for *Star Trek*?

2) What Federation ship was destroyed in the energy barrier at the edge of the universe?

3) Name the Enterprise crew member who gains superhuman powers when the ship passes through the energy barrier at the galaxy's edge.

4) On what planet does Kirk intend to maroon this dangerous superhuman crew member?

5) What facility on this planet can help in repairing the Enterprise's damaged warp drive?

6) Name the weapon that was introduced in this episode and never used again.

7) Who was the ship's resident psychiatrist?

8) What actor played the mutated superhuman crew member whom Kirk must destroy?

9) What physical changes are evident in this crew member that symbolize his growing powers?

10) What network accepted this pilot and when?

➤ The Series Takes Shape

1) What was the original name of Spock's native planet?

2) Who was the oldest person aboard the Enterprise?

3) What previous Gene Roddenberry TV series featured DeForest Kelley?

4) Which officers from the original *Star Trek* plans were dropped from the pilot for the first season?

5) What job did Sulu have before being assigned as helmsman?

6) Who played Yeoman Smith?

7) What physical feature of Spock's was air-brushed out of early publicity photos for the series?

8) Name the Enterprise's original helmsman.

9) Who played Yeoman Janice Rand?

10) Name the actor originally offered the role of Spock by Gene Roddenberry.

ANSWERS

➤ *Early Starts*

1) MGM

2) Robert T. April

3) He was half human, half Martian

4) First Lieutenant

5) Jose Ortegas from South America

6) Dr. Phillip Boyce

7) Number One

8) The S.S. Yorktown

9) The mission was to patrol the 9th quadrant, from Alpha Centauri to the outer limits of the Pinial Galaxy

10) Desilu Studios, who submitted it to NBC

➤ *First Pilot Episode*

1) The Cage

2) Leonard Nimoy and Majel Barrett

3) Jeffrey Hunter

4) Talos IV

5) The surface of the planet had been made uninhabitable in a nuclear war, the radiation from which rendered the population sterile

6) $630,000

7) It was never aired as filmed. Portions of it were used in a later episode, "The Menagerie"

8) To mate with a human from another starship so their children would repopulate the planet

9) S.S. Columbia

10) They took the elevator

➤ Second Pilot Episode

1) "Where no man has gone before"

2) Valiant

3) Lieutenant Commander Gary Mitchell

4) Delta Vega

5) An automated dilithium crystal cracking station

6) A phaser rifle

7) Dr. Elizabeth Dehner, played by Sally Kellerman

8) Gary Lockwood

9) His eyes glowed and his hair turned gray

10) NBC, February 1966

➤ *The Series Takes Shape*

1) Vulcanis
2) Dr. Mark Piper
3) Police Story
4) Dr. Piper, Yeoman Smith,
   Communications Officer Alden
5) Chief of astroscience department
6) Andrea Drom
7) His pointed ears
8) Lieutenant Phil Raintree
9) Grace Lee Whitney
10) DeForest Kelley

➤ Aboard the U.S.S. Enterprise

1) What class of starship is the Enterprise?

    A) Constellation
    B) Battle Cruiser
    C) Dreadnought
    D) Constitution
    E) Class J
    F) Explorer

2) What was the serial number of the original U.S.S. Enterprise?

3) What was the serial number of the Enterprise in *Star Trek: The Next Generation?*

4) What fuels the warp drive?

5) This substance, the only naturally occurring crystal with a helix-shaped pattern, buffers and controls power in the Enterprise and many of the devices used by Starfleet personnel.

6) What is the maximum speed the Enterprise can attain?

7) What prevents the crew of the Enterprise from floating around weightless in space, as the crews of current-day space missions do?

8) What is the Enterprise's primary mission?

9) How do the sensors operate?

10) Where do the phaser banks draw power from?

➤ Enterprise II

1) What type of explosion is responsible for the destructive force of a photon torpedo?

2) What are the three phaser settings?

3) Why does the Enterprise need a deflector?

4) How many shields does the Enterprise have?

5) What weapon is used to lock onto and pull or push objects?

6) Through what method can the Enterprise communicate with Starfleet headquarters at faster-than-light speeds?

7) How can communicators or phasers be turned into bombs?

8) How can the transporter locate a crew member for beam-up?

9) This device, built into the Enterprise's communications board, enables the bridge crew to communicate with non-English speaking aliens.

10) What sickbay device has built-in scanners and a read-out of the patient's vital signs displayed on a monitor?

➤ Enterprise III

1) On what date did the Enterprise return to Earth orbit following her last historic five-year mission?

2) How old was the Enterprise when returned to Earth for a major retrofit?

3) What was the class designation of the computer system in the original Enterprise?

4) What's the diameter of the saucer-shaped primary hull of the Enterprise?

5) How long are the nacelles containing the warp engines?

6) How long does it take the Enterprise to accelerate from zero miles per hour to light speed under impulse power?

7) How many people served aboard the Enterprise at any one time?

8) What company manufactured the warp engines of the original Enterprise?

9) In the retrofit Enterprise, what substance is used to generate the shields?

10) What is the safe beaming range for transporters?

➤ *Before the Enterprise...*

1) This DY-100 class sleeper ship left earth in 1996 with a crew of 97 genetically altered supermen.

2) Launched in 2002, it was the first interstellar probe designed to seek out new life forms.

3) When was the first warp-powered spaceship built and flown?

4) Name the first starship to reach the edge of the galaxy.

5) What class of starship had a bridge section that was sphere-shaped rather than saucer-shaped?

6) What weaponry did starships carry before phasers and photon torpedoes?

7) The starships of this race lack warp drives and travel at sublight speeds only.

8) Which aliens have starships equipped with cloaking devices that make them invisible?

9) What alien race has square spaceships?

10) They developed the powerful plasma-based weaponry.

➤ *Starships and Their Serial Numbers*

Match the starship in the numbered list with its serial number in the lettered list.

1) U.S.S. Enterprise
2) U.S.S. Hathaway
3) U.S.S. Excelsior
4) U.S.S. Bozeman
5) U.S.S. Stargazer
6) U.S.S. Tsiolkovsky
7) U.S.S. Victory
8) U.S.S. Hood H)
9) U.S.S. Phoenix
10) U.S.S. Excalibur

A) NCC-1941
B) NCC-59311
C) NCC-2893
D) NCC-9754
E) NCC-2593
F) NCC-65420
G) NCC-2000
H) NCC-26517

I) NCC-42296

J) NCC-1701

➤ *On Deck*

Match the facilities and systems in the numbered list with their location aboard the
Enterprise, given in the lettered list.

1) Main bridge

2) Security

3) Mess hall

4) Conference room

5) Senior officers' quarters

6) Impulse engineering

7) Sickbay

8) Auxiliary fire control

9) Primary hull circuit breaker

10) Main sensory array monitoring system

A) F Deck, Level 6

B) B Deck, Level 2

C) K Deck, Level 11

D) D Deck, Level 4

E) A Deck, Level 1

F) G Deck, Level 7

G) C Deck, Level 3

H) J Deck, Level 10

I) H–I Decks, Level 8–9

J) E Deck, Level 5

ANSWERS

➤ Aboard the U.S.S. Enterprise

1) D
2) NCC 1701
3) NCC 1701-D
4) An anti-matter/matter reaction
5) Dilithium crystals
6) Warp 12
7) Gravity generators
8) Research, exploration, mapping
9) Sensors measure reflected electromagnetic impulses
10) The main engines power the phaser banks

➤ Enterprise II

1) A matter/antimatter explosion
2) Stun, kill, destroy
3) Deflectors repel space dust and other small particles which, at the speed the Enterprise travels, could penetrate and damage the hull
4) Six
5) Tractor beams

6) Subspace communications

7) Set the dilithium crystals in phase and the devices will overload and explode

8) The transporter locks on to the crew member's communicator signal

9) The universal translator

10) Diagnostic bed

➤ *Enterprise III*

1) April 17, 2212

2) 25 years old

3) M-4

4) 460.5 feet

5) 12 seconds

6) 500—72 officers, 428 enlisted crew

7) Shuvinaalijis Warp Technologies

8) diburnium-osmium alloy

9) 19,500 miles

➤ *Before the Enterprise . . .*

1) S.S. Botany Bay

2) Nomad

3) 2061 AD

4) S.S. Valiant

5) Daedalus Class

6) Atomic missiles

7) Romulans

8) Romulans and Klingons

9) Borg

10) Romulans

➤ *Starships and Their Serial Numbers*

1) J

2) E

3) G

4) A

5) C

6) B

7) D

8) I

9) F

10) H

➤ *On Deck*

1) E

2) B

3) G

4) D

5) J

6) A

7) F

8) I

9) H

10) C

➤ Star Trek: Crew

1) Who is Kirk's yeoman?

2) What are McCoy's medical specialties?

3) Who was the youngest captain ever to command a starship?

4) Name the weapons officer and navigator of the Enterprise.

5) This Enterprise crew member is the son of Sarek and Amanda.

6) He was helmsman of the Enterprise and later captain of the Excelsior.

7) What is Uhuru's post aboard the Enterprise?

8) What is Scotty's first name?

9) What is McCoy's first name?

10) What is James T. Kirk's middle name?

11) What is Sulu's first name?

➤ Star Trek: Cast

1) James Doohan is a native of

    A) Scotland
    B) the U.S.A.
    C) Canada
    D) New Zealand
    E) Russia

2) Aside from *Star Trek*, on what other science fiction TV show was James Doohan offered the role of chief engineer?

3) This *Star Trek* actor served on the board of the Southern California Rapid Transit District.

4) What *Star Trek* cast member is of Lithuanian descent?

5) Which *Star Trek* cast member was a singer for Duke Ellington?

6) This *Star Trek* actor directed the film *Three Men and a Baby*.

7) Where was DeForest Kelley born?

8) Name the *Star Trek* cast member who appeared in the 1965 TV series "For the People."

9) This *Star Trek* cast member played the mermaid in Chicken of the Sea tuna TV commercials.

10) What *Star Trek* cast member guest-starred on the Batman TV series?

➤ *Star Trek: Supporting Cast*

Match the actor in the numbered list with the character played and the *Star Trek* episode he or she appeared in, listed in the lettered list.

1) Robert Walker Jr.
2) William Campbell
3) Lloyd Hanes
4) Roger C. Carmel
5) Robert Lansing
6) Vic Tayback
7) John Hoyt
8) James Gregory
9) Elisha Cooke Jr.
10) Glenn Corbett

A) Samuel T. Cogley, "Court Martial"
B) Zefram Cochrane, "Metamorphosis"
C) Charlie Evans, "Charlie X"
D) Harry Mudd, "I, Mudd"
E) Dr. Tristan Adams, "Dagger of the Mind"
F) Trevane, "The Squire of Gothos"
G) Gary Seven, "Assignment: Earth"
H) Krako, "A Piece of the Action"
I) Communications Officer Alden, "Where No Man Has Gone Before"
J) Dr. Philip Boyce, "The Cage"

➤ Star Trek: Guest Stars

Match the celebrity or actor in the numbered list with the character played and the *Star Trek* episode or film in which he or she appeared in the lettered list.

1) John Larroquette
2) Julie Newmar
3) Kirstie Alley
4) Barbara Babcock
5) Ted Cassidy
6) Teri Garr
7) Mariette Hartley
8) Jill Ireland
9) Joan Collins
10) Melvin Belli
11) Diana Muldaur
12) Christian Slater

A) Philana, "Plato's Stepchildren"
B) Ruk, "What are Little Girls Made Of?"
C) Edith Keeler, "The City on the Edge of Forever"
D) Maltz, "The Search for Spock"
E) Zarabeth, "All Our Yesterdays"
F) Eleen, "Friday's Child"
G) Gorgan, "And the Children Shall Lead"

H) Leila Kalum, "This Side of Paradise"

I) Roberta Lincoln, "Assignment: Earth"

J) Saavik, "The Wrath of Khan"

K) Starfleet officer, *Star Trek VI*

L) Dr. Ann Mulhall, "Return to Tomorrow"

➤ *Star Trek: Supporting Cast II*

Match the actor in the numbered list with the character played and the *Star Trek* episode he or she appeared in listed in the lettered list.

1) Clint Howard

2) Charlene Polite

3) Jan Shutan

4) Jan Shutan

5) Warren Stevens

6) Peter Brocco

7) Jeff Corey

8) Leslie Dalton

9) John Fiedler

10) Pamela Ferdin

A) Rojan, "By Any Other Name"

B) Plasus, "The Cloud Minders"

C) Jahn, "Miri"

D) Unnamed, "The Corbomite Maneuver"

E) Vanna, "The Cloud Minders"

F) Mary, "And the Children Shall Lead Them"

G) Claymare, "Errand of Mercy"

H) Hengist, "Wolf in the Fold"

I) Drea, "By Any Other Name"

J) Lt. Mira Romaine, "The Lights of Zetar"

➤ *Star Trek: The Next Generation: Crew*

1) Who is the chief engineer of the Enterprise?

2) What was Tasha Yar's original name?

3) Which crew member had the highest score on the Turing Test of sentience intelligence?

4) Wesley Crusher was originally supposed to be a girl. What was her name?

5) What device does blind LaForge wear that enables him to see?

6) Name the Klingon serving aboard the Enterprise.

7) This crew member has limited telepathic powers.

8) What year did Data graduate from Starfleet academy?

9) Which crew members wore miniskirts in the pilot episode?

10) What was Jean Luc Picard's original name?

➤ *Star Trek: The Next Generation: Cast I*

Match the crew member in the numbered list with the actor portraying him or her in the lettered list.

1) Captain Picard

2) Lt. Worf

3) Lt. Miles O'Brien

4) William Riker

5) Data

6) Lt. Deanna Troi

7) Tasha Yar

8) Geordi LaForge

9) Dr. Beverly Crusher

10) Wesley Crusher

A) Michael Dorn

B) Jonathan Frakes

C) Marina Sirtis

D) LeVar Burton

E) Patrick Stewart

F) Brent Spiner

G) Colm Meaney

H) Denise Crosby

I) Will Wheaton

J) Gates McFadden

➤ *Star Trek: The Next Generation: Cast II*

1) This *Star Trek: The Next Generation* cast member was a regular on "CHIPS."

2) Which *Next Generation* cast member played Gordie in the Stephen King/Rob Reiner film *Stand by Me?*

3) Name the *Next Generation* cast member who starred in the TV miniseries "Roots."

4) This *Next Generation* cast member has performed with the muppets.

5) Which *Next Generation* actor had a role in the daytime soap opera "Days of Our Lives"?

6) This *Next Generation* cast member played Sejanus in the TV miniseries "I, Claudius."

7) Aside from *Star Trek: The Next Generation,* this actor is best known for his role in the TV miniseries "North and South."

8) She appeared with Charles Bronson in the movie *Death Wish III.*

9) Which cast member appeared in Woody Allen's film *Stardust Memories?*

10) He played one of Apollo Creed's body-
    guards in *Rocky*.

➤ *Quotable Quotes*

Match the *Star Trek* actor in the numbered list
with his or her quote in the lettered list.

1) William Shatner

2) Leonard Nimoy

3) DeForest Kelley

4) James Doohan

5) Nichelle Nichols

6) Walter Koenig

7) Grace Lee Whitney

A) "I love all dialects."

B) "I'd wanted to be a doctor and couldn't—
   and yet became the most well-known
   doctor in the galaxy."

C) "I had no desire to get into show business,
   none at all."

D) "I think *Star Trek* is wonderful."

E) "You do the strange makeup, the ears,
   the eyebrows and the haircut. You go in
   and do what has to be done."

F) "Hollywood works in strange and totally
   unpredictable ways."

G) "I think an attempt was made to reduce me to a token black."

H) "Hallelujah to the *Star Trek* fans for sticking with us these 20 years."

I) "When I first began to be talked to about doing the series, a doctor gave me diet pills to lose 10 pounds."

ANSWERS

➤ Star Trek: Crew

1) Janice Rand
2) Surgery and space psychology
3) James Kirk
4) Pavel Chekhov
5) Spock
6) Sulu
7) Communications Officer
8) Montgomery
9) Leonard
10) Tiberius
11) Hikaru

➤ Star Trek: Cast

1) C
2) Voyage to the Bottom of the Sea
3) George Takei
4) Walter Koenig
5) Nichelle Nichols
6) Leonard Nimoy
7) Atlanta, Georgia
8) William Shatner

9) Grace Lee Whitney (she played Yeoman Rand in the first season)

10) Grace Lee Whitney

➤ *Star Trek: Supporting Cast*

1) C
2) F
3) I
4) D
5) G
6) H
7) J
8) E
9) A
10) B

➤ *Star Trek: Guest Stars*

1) D
2) F
3) J
4) A
5) B
6) I
7) E
8) H

9) C

10) G

11) L

12) K

➤ *Star Trek: Supporting Cast II*

1) D

2) E

3) C

4) J

5) A

6) G

7) B

8) I

9) H

10) F

➤ *Star Trek: The Next Generation: Crew*

1) Lt. Geordi LaForge

2) Macha Hernandez

3) Data

4) Leslie Crusher

5) VISOR (Visual Instrument and Sight Organ Replacement)

6) Lt. Worf

7) Lt. Deanna Troi

8) 2338 AD

9) Deanna Troi and Tasha Yar

10) Julien Picard

➤ *Star Trek: The Next Generation: Cast I*

1) E

2) A

3) G

4) B

5) F

6) C

7) H

8) D

9) J

10) I

➤ *Star Trek: The Next Generation: Cast II*

1) Michael Dorn

2) Will Wheaton

3) LeVar Burton

4) Gates McFadden

5) Denise Crosby

6) Patrick Stewart

7) Jonathan Frakes

8) Marina Sirtis

9) Brent Spiner

10) Michael Dorn

➤ *Quotable Quotes*

1) D

2) E

3) B

4) A, C

5) G

6) H

7) I

➤ *First Season I*

1) What substance does the vampire-like creature M-113 extract from its victims' bodies?

2) What was the name for the Federation before it was called Starfleet Command?

3) Who played the Romulan ship captain who has attacked Federation bases in the neutral zone with a plasma energy weapon?

4) What cripples and disfigures Spock's former commanding officer, Captain Christopher Pike?

5) What race of beings gives human Charlie X his telekinetic powers?

6) What actress supplied the voice of the Enterprise's computer?

7) Name the penal colony on which inmates take over and use a neural neutralizer on Kirk.

8) This actor performing on Planet Q is really Kodos the Executioner.

9) What oath does Kirk help Tyree recite in "A Private Little War"?

10) Name the three types of propulsion systems used by the Enterprise

➤ First Season II

1) Kirk is accused of negligent homicide in the death of this Enterprise crewman.

2) Spock is promoted from what to what in the second season?

3) What crime is Spock court-martialed for?

4) He is known as the "Squire of Gothos."

5) Kirk fights the lizard captain of an alien starship on Cestus III. What is the name of this alien race?

6) Name the planet, dominated by women, where technicians repairing the Enterprise's computer gave the system a female voice.

7) How does the Enterprise accidentally get propelled back to the year 1969?

8) What computer became the ruler of planet Beta III by incorporating inhabitants into "the body"?

9) Name the spaceship in which Khan is found in suspended animation.

10) The son of this U.S. Air Force captain led
    the first successful Earth-Saturn probe.

➤ *First Season III*

1) What was the average budget for a *Star
   Trek* episode?

2) Which of these science fiction writers were
   members of the Committee formed to
   save *Star Trek* from cancellation?

   A) A.E. Van Vogt
   B) Ray Bradbury
   C) Isaac Asimov
   D) Phillip K. Dick
   E) Arthur C. Clarke
   F) Frank Herbert

3) What self-destruct system does Kirk
   threaten to activate to destroy the
   Fesarius, a giant ship that has trapped the
   Enterprise?

4) What cargo does Harry Mudd carry?

5) How is Kirk split into two beings (a good
   Kirk and an evil Kirk)?

6) Nickname given to Dr. McCoy by archae-
   ologist Nancy Crater, an old flame.

7) Name the actor who played Lieutenant
   Kevin Thomas Riley.

8) On what planet did members of the
   Enterprise crew contract a disease which

caused them to lose control of their inner personalities?

9) Who was Nurse Chapel engaged to before falling in love with Mr. Spock?

10) On what planet do Spock, McCoy and Scotty crash-land in the shuttlecraft Galileo?

➤ *First Season IV*

1) Which planets fought a war with computer simulations, in which casualties allow themselves to be destroyed in anti-matter chambers to prevent an all-out, "real" war?

2) Name the botanist with whom Spock falls in love when alien plant spores on planet Omicron Ceti III cause him to allow his emotions to be released.

3) What silicon-based life form can burrow through solid stone?

4) What is the Vulcan credo?

5) This race of superior energy beings prevents war between the Federation and the Klingons.

6) What device sends McCoy, Spock and Kirk back in time to 1930s Earth?

7) Name the "Dynasty" star who plays social worker Edith Keeler.

8) You know the difference between Vulcan and human ears. What is the difference between Vulcan and human eyes?

9) He was a madman from an antimatter universe who planned to invade our galaxy.

10) What are Sulu's favorite hobbies?

ANSWERS

➤ *First Season I*

1) Salt

2) Star Fleet Control or the United Earth Space Probe Agency (UESPA)

3) Mark Lenard, who went on to play Sarek, Spock's father

4) Exposure to delta-rays during a starship accident

5) The Thasians

6) Majel Barrett, who also played Nurse Chapel and was later married to Gene Roddenberry

7) Tantalus V

8) Anton Karidian

9) The Pledge of Allegiance

10) Thrusters, impulse drive, warp drive

➤ *First Season II*

1) Records Officer Ben Finney

2) He is promoted from lieutenant commander to commander

3) Kidnapping Captain Christopher Pike, commandeering the Enterprise to planet Talos IV, sabotage and attempted violation of General Order 7

4) Trelane

5) The Gorns

6) Cygnet XIV

7) When using reverse warp drive to avoid collision with a black hole

8) Landru

9) S.S. Botany Bay

10) Captain John Christopher

➤ *First Season III*

1) $180,000

2) A, F

3) Corbomite

4) Women made beautiful using an illegal drug from Venus

5) A transporter malfunction splits Kirk into two beings

6) Plum

7) Bruce Hyde

8) Psi 2000

9) Dr. Roger Korby

10) Taurus II

➤ *First Season IV*

1) Eminiar and Vendikar

2) Leila Kalomi

3) The Horta

4) "Infinite diversity in infinite combinations"

5) The Organians

6) The Guardian of Forever

7) Joan Collins

8) Vulcans have an extra eyelid to protect them from the harsh Vulcan sun

9) Lazarus

10) Botany and fencing

➤ Second Season I

1) What is the name of the baby Dr. McCoy delivers on Capella IV?

2) What is the Vulcan term for the seven-year mating cycle to which all male Vulcans are subject?

3) This well-known actor played Commander Matt Decker.

4) Who is Spock's Vulcan fiancee?

5) What is the Vulcan ceremony for challenge of the right of marriage?

6) Scotty is accused of murders actually committed by this energy being.

7) Kirk destroys this space probe, which has killed billions of people in carrying out its mission to sterilize alien life forms.

8) The natives of Gamma Trianguli VI

sacrifice themselves to provide fuel for this godlike computer.

9) What caused the Enterprise landing party to switch places with their counterparts from a parallel universe ruled by violence?

10) What is the key ingredient of Dr. McCoy's cure for hyperaccelerated aging disease?

➤ *Second Season II*

1) What space station becomes overrun with tribbles?

2) Name the hybrid wheat the tribbles have infested.

3) On which planet has the civilization developed a Roman gladiator culture with 20th century Earth technology?

4) What health condition does Sarek suffer?

5) On what planet do the Klingons, Romulans and the Federation establish a joint colony?

6) Aliens on the planet Triskelion force Kirk, Uhura and Chekhov to wear obedience collars, turning them into this kind of slave.

7) Which Federation starship had an all-Vulcan crew?

8) Name three aliens whose intellects are contained in spheres.

9) What Star Fleet cultural observer becomes a Nazi dictator on the planet Ekos?

10) He invented the M-5 multitronic computer.

➤ Second Season III

1) What major character was introduced in the second season?

2) Who was the producer of *Star Trek* in the second season?
   A) Gene Roddenberry
   B) Gene Coon
   C) John Meredyth
   D) Robert Justman
   E) Aaron Spelling

3) She used the transmuter wand to change herself into a giant black cat. And, she had a crush on Kirk.

4) Who invented the space warp drive?

5) This alien once lived on Mount Olympus and was believed by the Greeks to be a god.

6) What is the Vulcan term for the blood fever caused by the Vulcan mating cycle?

7) Name the giant cylinder that destroys planets and cripples the U.S.S. Constellation.

8) Who controls the androids in "I, Mudd"?

9) Who wrote the *Star Trek* episode "The Trouble with Tribbles"?

10) Name the species of white horned gorilla that poisons Kirk with its bite.

➤ *Second Season IV*

1) What form of currency do The Providers wager when they pit Kirk, Uhura and Chekhov against alien gladiators in combat games?

2) Who was Kirk's captain aboard the U.S.S. Farragut?

3) What actor played crew member Mr. Leslie?

4) Which solar system was wiped out by the giant space amoeba in "The Immunity Syndrome"?

5) This civilization patterned itself after the Chicago gangster mobs of the roaring '20s.

6) Who takes over the Enterprise by turning most of the crew members into small tetrahedral blocks?

7) The M-5 computer goes haywire and kills the crew of this starship in practice maneuvers.

8) The crew of this starship is reduced to crystallized powder by a deadly virus.

9) This time traveler is immune to the Vulcan nerve pinch.

10) Name the Asian race on planet Omega IV that patterned itself after the Communist party.

ANSWERS

➤ *Second Season I*

1) Leonard James Akaar

2) pon farr

3) William Windom

4) T'Pring

5) Koon-ut-kal-if-fee

6) Redjac

7) Nomad

8) Vaal

9) A transporter disruption causes the switch

10) adrenaline

➤ *Second Season II*

1) Space station K-7

2) quadrotriticale

3) 892-IV

4) He has a heart condition and has suffered two mild heart attacks

5) Nimbus III

6) Thralls

7) U.S.S. Intrepid

8) Henoch, Sargon and Thalassa

9) John Gill

10) Dr. Richard Daystrom

► *Second Season III*

1) Ensign Pavel Chekhov
2) C
3) Sylvia
4) Zefram Cochrane
5) Apollo
6) plak tow
7) A berserker
8) Norman
9) David Gerrold
10) A mugatu

► *Second Season IV*

1) Kwat-loos
2) Garrovick
3) Eddie Paskey
4) Gamma 7A
5) The Lotians
6) The Kelvans, led by Rojan
7) Excalibur
8) Exeter
9) Gary Seven
10) The Khoms

➤ Third Season I

1) What power do members of the Melkot race possess?

2) Name the tribal woman whom Kirk marries.

3) What is the proper designation for an Earth-type planet?

4) Her tears contain a chemical that makes men fall in love with her.

5) What famous attorney played Gorgan the Friendly Angel?

6) Who stole Spock's brain by surgically removing it from his body?

7) She is blind but can "see" thanks to a metallic dress containing a sensor web.

8) The sight of members of this alien race drives men insane.

9) Who tortured McCoy as part of an experiment?

10) The crew of this starship captain mutinied when he ordered them to kill the inhabitants of planet Antos IV.

➤ *Third Season II*

1) What spatial phenomenon is caused by the temporary overlap of two universes?

2) He looks like a crystal with eyes.

3) What rare blood disorder is McCoy stricken with?

4) This ship, which attacks the Enterprise with missiles, looks like a giant asteroid.

5) What alien woman does McCoy marry?

6) What mineral gives Kirk and Spock temporary telekinetic powers on the planet Platonius?

7) What leader of Platonius attempts to force McCoy to stay with him as his private doctor?

8) What catastrophe caused genetic damage to the Scalosians, resulting in sterility of the males and a hyperaccelerated metabolism that makes them superfast and invisible to the naked eye?

9) The last surviving member of the Kalandan colony, her computer-generated image remains part of the uninhabited colony's automated defense system.

10) Lokai from Cheron, played by Frank Gorshin, is half black and half white. Which half is black?

➤ *Third Season III*

1) What is the name of the crawl space through which Enterprise engineers gain access to the warp drives and other internal mechanisms?

2) Once romantically involved with Kirk, she used alien technology to transfer her consciousness to his body so she could take over the Enterprise.

3) Name McCoy's daughter. What is her profession?

4) What former starship captain uses a cellular metamorphosis technique to change his appearance at will?

5) Kirk contracted but survived this virulent disease.

6) Why is the planet Gideon so overpopulated that there is literally standing room only?

7) What is the name of the Federation's central library facility?

8) Name the cloud city of planet Ardana.

9) Name the Ardana surface dwellers working in the mines.

10) What rare element is found on Ardana?

➤ *Third Season IV*

1) Chekhov was romantically involved with this woman who boards the Enterprise on her way to planet Eden.

2) Name the immortal Earth man who lived for thousands of years assuming a variety of identities that included Brahms and da Vinci.

3) It's the only known cure for Rigellian Fever.

4) Who was the Vulcan who created and spread the philosophy of suppressed emotions?

5) When a time portal sends him back to her planet's Ice Age, Spock falls in love with this woman.

6) Who is the librarian of Sarpeidon?

7) She is possessed by energy composed of the last survivors of Zetar.

8) On what planet does Kirk meet a being claiming to be Abraham Lincoln?

9) To what planet does an energy being lure the Enterprise and a Klingon battle cruiser commanded by Kang?

10) The chief officer from Cheron, his mission is to hunt down Lokai.

ANSWERS

➤ *Third Season I*

1) telepathy
2) Miramanee
3) Class M
4) Elaan, the Dohlman of Elas
5) Melvin Belli
6) Kara of Sigma Draconis VI
7) Dr. Miranda Jones
8) The Medusans
9) The Vians
10) Garth

➤ *Third Season II*

1) Interphase
2) Commander Loskane of the Tholian Assembly
3) xeno-polycythemia
4) Yonada
5) Yonadan high priestess Natira
6) kironide
7) Parmen

8) Genetic damage was caused by radiation emitted from the planet's core and released by volcanic activity

9) Losira

10) His right side is black; his left side, white

➤ *Third Season III*

1) The Jeffries Tube

2) Dr. Janice Lester

3) Joanna McCoy, who is a nurse.

4) Garth of Izar

5) Vegan choriomeningitis

6) There is no disease on the planet

7) Memory Alpha

8) Stratos

9) Troglytes

10) Zienite

➤ *Third Season: IV*

1) Irini Galliulin

2) Flint

3) Ryetalyn

4) Surak

5) Zarabeth

6) Mr. Atoz

7) Mira Romaine

8) Excalibur

9) Beta XII-A

10) Bele

➤ *Professional Life*

1) Who did Gene Roddenberry call before William Shatner and ask to play Captain Kirk?

2) What science fiction TV series, before *Star Trek*, did Shatner appear in?

3) In what Broadway play did Shatner appear with Spencer Tracy prior to the filming of the first *Star Trek* pilot?

4) What TV pilot did Shatner appear in prior to the filming of the second *Star Trek* pilot?

5) Which of these avocations does William Shatner enjoy?

    A) novelist
    B) breeder of champion horses
    C) dog fancier
    D) flying
    E) comic book writer

6) What popular TV show has Shatner guest-hosted in which he played himself?

7) Name Shatner's daughter, who appeared with him in a TV commercial and the movie *Star Trek V*.

8) When was William Shatner born?

9) What was Shatner's first film?

10) Aside from *Star Trek*, what other TV series has Shatner starred in?

➤ *Star Trek Memories*

1) In which body part did George Takei accidentally stab William Shatner in "The Naked Time"?

2) Whose bicycle did William Shatner steal repeatedly on the set of *Star Trek*?

3) What kind of car did Shatner drive during the first season of *Star Trek*?

4) What are the titles of the novels written by William Shatner?

5) What comic book series did Shatner help create?

6) Who is Shatner's fiction collaborator?

7) Which *Star Trek* cast member allegedly refuses to talk to Shatner?

8) Which *Star Trek* camera operator did

Shatner ride dirt bikes with in the California desert?

9) Name the first regular (nonpilot) *Star Trek* episode starring Shatner.

10) On a "Twilight Zone" episode, Shatner's character stops for lunch in a diner. What does he order?

ANSWERS

➤ *Professional Life*

1) Jack Lord

2) "Twilight Zone," "The Outer Limits"

3) *Judgment at Nuremberg*

4) Alexander the Great

5) A, B, C, D, E

6) "Saturday Night Live"

7) Melanie Shatner

8) March 22, 1931

9) *The Brothers Karamazov*

10) "Barbary Coast," "T.J. Hooker," "Rescue 911"

➤ *Star Trek Memories*

1) His left nipple

2) Leonard Nimoy's

3) Corvette Stingray

4) *Tek Wars, Tek Lord*

5) *Tek Wars*

6) Ron Goulert

7) James Doohan

8) Al Francis

9) "Corbomite Manuever"

10) A lettuce and tomato sandwich

➤ *The Life and Times of Leonard Nimoy*

1) What is the title of Leonard Nimoy's autobiography?

2) Which of the following artistic endeavors has Nimoy been active in?

    A) movie directing
    B) poetry
    C) record albums
    D) writing
    E) stage acting

3) Who is Nimoy's ex-wife?

4) Name Nimoy's two children.

5) In what 1952 science fiction film did Nimoy play the alien Narab?

6) In which of the following TV shows did Nimoy guest-star?

    A) "Gunsmoke"
    B) "Dragnet"
    C) "The Lieutenant"
    D) "Get Smart"

E) "The Dick Van Dyke Show"
F) "The Outer Limits"

7) Of which *Star Trek* movie was Nimoy executive producer?

8) Which of the *Star Trek* movies did Nimoy direct?

9) Which *Star Trek* movie did Nimoy help write?

10) In what science fiction movie did Nimoy play a soldier fighting giant ants?

ANSWERS

➤ *The Life and Times of Leonard Nimoy*

1) *I am Not Spock*
2) A, B, C, D, E
3) Sandi Zober
4) Julie and Adam
5) *Zombies of the Stratosphere*
6) A, B, C, D, F
7) *Star Trek VI*
8) *Star Trek III* and *IV*
9) *Star Trek IV*
10) *Them*

➤ *What's Up Doc*

1) What did DeForest Kelley do for a living before he became an actor?

2) What was his first acting job?

3) In what film did Kelley play a Paramount talent scout?

4) What type of film did Kelley most frequently appear in?

5) On what TV western did Kelley guest star as a doctor?

6) On what TV show did Kelley play a doctor in communication with a UFO in distress?

7) In what city and year was Kelley born?

8) Who is Kelley married to?

9) What does Kelley do for a living today?

10) What is his hobby?

➤ *The Doctor is In*

1) Name the studio executive who rejected Kelley as Veronica Lake's costar in *This Gun for Hire*.

2) Which two movie studios were the first to offer Kelley a contract?

3) What was Kelley's first feature film?

4) In which of these TV series has Kelley appeared?
   A)"Wanted Dead or Alive"
   B) "You Are There"
   C) "Studio One"
   D) "The Web"
   E) "The Big Story"

5) DeForest Kelley acted in this radio serial that involved a doctor.

6) What was the first Gene Roddenberry TV project in which Kelley appeared?

7) In what movie did Kelley play villain Amos True?

8) Does Kelley prefer to play a good guy or a bad guy?

9) Which of these TV pilots featured Kelley?
   A) "Rawhide"
   B) "Two Faces West"
   C) "Bonanza"
   D) "True Grit"
   E) "Daddy's Girl"

10) On what TV show did Kelley once play a drunken doctor who lets Leonard Nimoy's character die?

ANSWERS

➤ What's Up Doc

1) He was a singer with the Lew Forbes Orchestra

2) He appeared in a U.S. Army training film during World War II

3) *Variety Girl*

4) Westerns

5) "Bonanza"

6) "Y.O.R.D.," an episode of the "Science Fiction Theatre"

7) Atlanta, Georgia, 1920

8) Carolyn Dowling

9) He is retired

10) He grows prize roses

➤ The Doctor is In

1) Bill Meiklejohn

2) Paramount and Columbia

3) "Fear in the Night"

4) A, B, C, D, E

5) "The Doctor's Wife"

6) "333 Montgomery," broadcast on the Alcoa Goodyear Theatre

7) "Gunfight at Comanche Creek"

8) The bad guy

9) A, B

10) "The Virginian"

➤ *Takei One*

1) Where was George Takei born?

2) In what city was Takei's father born?

3) What award did Takei win at Mount Vernon Junior High School for academic service and achievement?

4) For what organization did George Takei do volunteer work while in high school?

5) What was Takei's sport in high school?

6) In what film did Takei appear with Richard Burton?

7) Takei appeared in this film, which was the first to deal with the internment of Japanese–Americans in camps during World War II.

8) In what did George Takei invest the money he made from his first acting job in the movies?

    A) race horses
    B) pork bellies

C) U.S. savings bonds

D) cemetery plots

E) acting lessons

9) George Takei appeared with Alec Guiness in this film, made from a Broadway play.

10) Name the two Jerry Lewis films in which Takei appears.

➤ Takei Two

1) After the Japanese attack on Pearl Harbor, Takei and his family were relocated to this camp for the internment of Japanese–Americans.

2) Name the episode of Playhouse 90 that marked Takei's first appearance on television.

3) Where did Takei go to college and what was his major?

4) In what Broadway musical did Takei appear?

5) On which of these TV shows has Takei guest-starred?

A) "Twilight Zone"

B) "My Three Sons"

C) "Lassie"

D) "McHale's Navy"

E) "Bonanza"

6) In what film did Takei appear with fellow

Star Trek actor Jeffrey Hunter (the original captain of the Enterprise)?

7) In what film did Takei appear with John Wayne?

8) In what film did Takei appear with Cary Grant?

9) In what film did Takei appear with James Caan?

10) What Los Angeles mayor asked George Takei to sit on the board of directors of the Southern California Rapid Transit Authority?

ANSWERS

➤ Takei One

1) San Francisco, CA

2) Yamanashi, Japan

3) The American Legion Award

4) The Junior Red Cross

5) Track and field

6) *Ice Palace*

7) *Hell to Eternity*

8) D

9) *A Majority of One*

10) *The Big Mouth* and *Which Way to the Front?*

➤ Takei Two

1) Rohwer Relocation Center, Block 6

2) "Made in Japan"

3) He majored in theater at UCLA.

4) *Fly Blackbird!*

5) A, B

6) *Hell to Eternity*

7) *The Green Berets*

8) *Walk, Don't Run*

9) *Red Line 7000*

10) Tom Bradley

➤ First Season

1) How old is Dr. Leonard McCoy when he visits the U.S.S. Enterprise at Farpoint Station?

2) This pesky superbeing interfered with many of Picard's missions, including the one at Farpoint.

3) Name the Ferengi who tried to frame Captain Picard for the destruction of the U.S.S. Stargazer.

4) He is the roboticist who designed and built Data.

5) Name Data's twin brother.

6) What alien creature killed Enterprise Security Chief Tasha Yar on planet Vagra II?

7) Where was Jean-Luc Picard born?

8) Which member of the Enterprise crew was rejected the first time he applied to Star Fleet Academy?

9) This "My Favorite Martian" star plays Boothby, the Star Fleet Academy groundskeeper.

10) From what alien race is Counselor Deanna Troi?

➤ Second Season

1) What was the name of the computer-generated, self-aware life form created accidentally by the holodeck?

2) In which star system does the Enterprise make first contact with a Borg spacecraft?

3) An alien plant seriously injures commander William Riker on this planet.

4) Name the judge who ruled that Data is a life form and therefore has the same civil rights as any human.

5) Guinan, played by comedienne Whoopie Goldberg, is the hostess of which lounge aboard the U.S.S. Enterprise?

6) He replaced Tasha Yar as chief security officer of the Enterprise.

7) Which doctor replaces Beverly Crusher as the chief medical officer of the Enterprise?

8) Under whose command and on what ship did Geordi LaForge serve with prior to Picard and the Enterprise?

9) To which Klingon ship in the Federation is Riker temporarily reassigned?

10) With which Klingon emissary did

Lieutenant Worf have an affair and a child?

➤ *Third Season*

1) Miniature robotic devices designed for medical applications evolve into a new life form aboard the Enterprise. What is this race called?

2) Name the alien superbeing who destroys an entire species, the Husnock, on planet Delta Rana IV.

3) Which "L.A. Law" star played a member of the Q continuum?

4) A half Romulan and half human, she is Tasha Yar's daughter and a Romulan operative.

5) The name Data gives to the android child he builds.

6) What charge is brought by the Klingon High Council against Worf's biological father?

7) She was Sarek's second wife, after Amanda.

8) She is the Federation officer in charge of developing a defense strategy against the Borg.

9) What devastatingly powerful alien weapon is unearthed by Picard on an archaeological dig during his shore leave?

10) A former member of TV's "The A-Team" played this systems diagnostics engineer assigned to the U.S.S. Enterprise.

➤ Fourth Season

1) What casualties do the Federation suffer during the Wolf 359 battle with the Borg?

2) When Picard was made into a Borg, what was he called?

3) Name Worf's adoptive Earth parents.

4) He is the Enterprise's transporter chief.

5) Name Worf's son.

6) Name Data's pet cat.

7) Which member of the Enterprise crew has his intelligence increased 100-fold when exposed to radiation from an alien probe?

8) This star of the "MASH" TV series played Kaelon scientist Timicin.

9) A security officer, she has a romantic relationship with Data.

10) What position does Worf take upon resigning from Star Fleet?

➤ Fifth Season

1) Which "Cheers" star plays Captain Morgan Bateson of the U.S.S. Bozeman?

2) Name the Borg boy rescued by the Enterprise.

3) This former "Max Headroom" star played time traveler Professor Berlinghoff Rasmussen.

4) Riker temporarily assumes command of this Ambassador-class starship.

5) She is a botanist aboard the Enterprise and married to Chief O'Brien.

6) What alien race attempted to gain control of Star Fleet by getting Star Fleet personnel addicted to a video game?

7) How old was Sarek when he died?

8) What dangerous spacecraft maneuver caused a serious flight accident involving Wesley Crusher and four of his fellow Star Fleet Academy cadets?

9) The Enterprise attempts to save an enclosed biosphere on this planet from collision with a stellar core fragment.

10) Name the planet destroyed by the Crystalline Entity.

► Sixth Season

1) What famous author does Picard meet in "Time's Arrow"?

2) What crew member from the original Enterprise is beamed aboard the new

Enterprise after being trapped in a transporter loop for 75 years?

3) Who plays the new Enterprise captain when Picard is sent on an espionage mission?

4) Which crew member turns into a Romulan?

5) What ancient Klingon leader is biologically resurrected?

6) Who directed the episode "Time Scape"?

7) After years of being emotionless, what emotion does Data finally display?

8) In what century does the action on the show take place?

9) How did the woman who comes aboard the Enterprise with almost godlike powers gain her powers?

10) Where does Worf lead an informant promising to lead him to his father?

ANSWERS

➤ First Season

1) 137 years old
2) Q
3) DaiMon Bok
4) Dr. Noonien Soong
5) Lore
6) Armus
7) LeBarre, France
8) Captain Picard
9) Ray Walston
10) Betazoid

➤ Second Season

1) Moriarty
2) System J-25
3) Surata IV
4) Judge Advocate General Phillipa Louvois
5) Ten Forward Lounge
6) Lieutenant Worf
7) Dr. Katherine Palaski
8) Captain Zimbata, Starship Victory
9) Pagh
10) K'Ehleyr

➤ Third Season

1) Nanites

2) Douwd

3) Corbin Bernsen

4) Sela

5) Lal (which is Hindi for beloved)

6) He is charged with being a traitor for his role in the Khitomer Massacre

7) Perrin

8) Lieutenant Commander Shelby

9) Tox Uthat

10) Lieutenant Reginald Barclay III

➤ Fourth Season

1) 11,000 personnel, 39 starships

2) Locutus of Borg

3) Serge and Helena Rozhenko

4) Miles Edward O'Brien

5) Alexander Rozhenko

6) Spot

7) Lieutenant Reginald Barclay III

8) David Ogden Stiers

9) Jenna D'Sora

10) Weapons officer aboard the Klingon attack cruiser Bortas

➤ Fifth Season

1) Kelsey Grammer

2) Hugh Borg

3) Matt Frewer

4) Excalibur

5) Keiko

6) The Ktarans

7) 203 years old

8) A Kolvoord Starburst

9) Moab IV

10) Melona IV

➤ Sixth Season

1) Samuel Clemens

2) Scotty

3) Ronny Cox (star of *Beverly Hills Cop* and *Robocop*)

4) Deanna Troi

5) Kahless

6) Adam Nimoy, Leonard Nimoy's son

7) Anger

8) The 24th century

9) Her father was a member of the Q race

10) Deep Space Nine space station

➤ Crew

1) How did Commander Sisko's wife die?

2) What officer aboard Deep Space Nine is a former terrorist?

3) At what age did Lt. Julian Bashire graduate from Starfleet Medical Academy?

4) Which crew member consists of two entities, a host and a symbiont?

5) Which crew member served as transporter chief under Captain Jean Luc Picard aboard the Enterprise?

6) What is Security Chief Odo's special power?

7) Who operates the bar and gambling emporium aboard Deep Space Nine?

8) What is Sisko's son's rank?

9) Who starts a school for children aboard Deep Space Nine?

10) What crime did Quark's nephew Nog commit?

➤ Cast

Match the Deep Space Nine crew member in the numbered list with the actor who plays him or her in the lettered list.

1) Dr. Julian Bashir
2) Lt. Jadzia Dax
3) Major Kira Neyrs
4) Operations Chief Miles O'Brien
5) Security Chief Odo
6) Quark
7) Commander Ben Sisko
8) Keiko O'Brien
9) Jake Sisko
10) Ensign Ro

A) Cirroc Lofton
B) Rosalind Chao
C) Avery Brooks
D) Armin Shimmerman
E) Rene Auberjonois
F) Terry Farrell
G) Nana Visitor
H) Siddig El Fadil

I) Colm Meaney

J) Michelle Forbes

➤ *Deep Space Nine I*

1) What is Deep Space Nine?

2) Where is Deep Space Nine located?

3) Who built Deep Space Nine?

4) Where does Odo believe he's from?

5) Which crew member was found as an infant floating in space in a ship emerging from the wormhole?

6) What year is *Deep Space Nine* set in?

7) Who created the series?

8) What was the major industry of Bajor under the Cardassians?

9) Who is Bajor's spiritual leader?

10) What is "pagh"?

➤ *Deep Space Nine II*

1) What is Deep Space Nine's equivalent of the Enterprise's bridge called?

2) Where does computer-simulated sex take place?

3) Who is Quark's best customer at the bar?

4) What color skin do Bolins have?

5) Which *Deep Space Nine* cast member played the Ferengi Letek on *Star Trek: The Next Generation*?

6) Which Deep Space Nine crew member killed a Cardassian in hand-to-hand combat—his only act of physical violence?

7) For how long did Cardassians rule Bajor?

8) You can instantly travel from the Alpha to the Gamma Quadrants through the wormhole. How long would it take to make the trip at warp speed?

9) What is the population of Deep Space Nine?

10) What device is attached to starships to enable them to travel through the wormhole safely?

➤ *Deep Space Nine III*

1) What is the maximum warp speed a Runabout Class Ship can reach?

2) What is the main walkway of Deep Space Nine called?

3) What shape dominates Bajoran architecture?

4) What *Deep Space Nine* cast member played Hawk on the TV series *Spencer for Hire*?

5) What is a Trill?

6) Which *Deep Space Nine* cast member was a model in real life and played a model in the TV series "Paper Dolls," in which Jonathan Frakes costarred?

7) Which *Deep Space Nine* cast member was a regular on the soap opera "One Life to Live"?

8) What is the best planet for gambling in the galaxy?

9) What *Deep Space Nine* cast member was a regular on the TV series "Benson"?

10) Where is the Ferengi's erogenous zones located?

ANSWERS

➤ Crew

1) She was killed by the Borg at the Wolf 359 massacre
2) Major Kira
3) Age 26
4) Lt. Jadzia Dax
5) Chief Miles O'Brien
6) He is a shape-shifter
7) Quark, a Ferengi
8) Jake Sisko is an ensign
9) Keiko O'Brien, Chief O'Brien's wife
10) Commander Sisko caught him trying to steal ore samples

➤ Cast

1) H
2) F
3) G
4) I
5) E
6) D
7) C
8) B

9) A

10) J

➤ *Deep Space Nine I*

1) A space station

2) In orbit around planet Bajor in the Alpha Quadrant

3) The Cardassians

4) Gamma Quadrant

5) Odo

6) 2360 AD

7) Michael Piller and Rick Berman

8) Mining

9) Kai Opaka

10) A person's energy aura

➤ *Deep Space Nine II*

1) Command/Ops Center

2) holo-suites

3) Lurian

4) blue

5) Armin Shimmerman

6) Chief O'Brien

7) 40 years

8) 60 years traveling at warp factor 9

9) 200 residents and 50 Starfleet officers and crew members

10) An impulse energy buffer is required so that the ship's engines do not destroy the ionic field inside the wormhole

➤ *Deep Space Nine III*

1) Warp factor 4.7

2) The Promenade

3) A sphere

4) Avery Brooks

5) A worm-like symbiont in a humanoid host

6) Terry Farrell

7) Nana Visitor

8) Alphard V

9) Rene Auberjonois

10) Their ears

➤ *Star Trek: The Motion Picture*

1) Who was the new captain of the U.S.S. Enterprise?

2) What was Kirk's rank in Star Fleet at the star date when this adventure began?

3) Name the Vulcan state of perfection Spock tried and failed to attain.

4) How can Kirk legally draft the semiretired McCoy back into active duty with Star Fleet?

5) What alien entity threatening the Earth did Kirk have to find a way to stop?

6) She was the new navigator of the Enterprise and was turned into a robotic probe by the alien.

7) What was the origin of the alien entity?

8) How does Spock communicate with the alien?

9) What was the alien's mission?

10) What crew member merges with the alien, giving it emotions?

➤ *Star Trek II: The Wrath of Khan*

1) What "Cheers" star played Vulcan Lieutenant Saavik?

2) What is Khan's full name?

3) On which planet had Kirk marooned Khan and his followers?

4) Name the parasite Khan uses to control Chekhov's mind.

5) Kirk had a temporary marriage contract (arrangement) with this woman.

6) Which Federation ship does Khan seize control of?

7) What secret Federation project does Khan steal?

8) Spock transfers this part of his being to McCoy shortly before he dies of radiation exposure.

9) Kirk lures Khan and his crew into this gaseous body in which ships' shields and screens do not operate.

10) He is the son Kirk never knew he had.

➤ *Star Trek III: The Search for Spock*

1) Why does Kirk steal the Enterprise to

make an unauthorized trip to the Genesis planet?

2) This "Hill Street Blues" star plays the captain of the U.S.S. Excelsior.

3) You know the Enterprise's serial number. What is the Excelsior's serial number?

4) The Excelsior is equipped with this new type of warp drive.

5) This "Taxi" star plays Klingon Commander Kruge.

6) Name Kruge's second-in-command, whom Kirk tricks into beaming him and Spock aboard the Klingon ship.

7) Which *Star Trek* cast member directed *Star Trek III?*

8) This Vulcan high priestess helps restore Spock to normal.

9) What is the Vulcan process for re-fusing Spock's spirit into his living body?

10) What type of Klingon vessel do Kirk and crew hijack?

➤ *Star Trek IV: The Voyage Home*

1) Who directed *Star Trek IV?*

2) Where is the headquarters of the United Federation of Planets located?

3) What name does McCoy give the Klingon

ship the Enterprise crew uses to return to Earth from Vulcan?

4) What life form is the giant alien probe searching for on Earth?

5) How is Kirk and his crew able to travel backward in time to the 20th century?

6) Where in 20th century Earth does Kirk "park" the stolen Klingon ship?

7) Name the two whales Kirk plans to transport back to the 23rd century aboard the Klingon vessel.

8) The formula for this material is given by Scotty to Dr. Nichols in exchange for plexiglass with which to construct a whale tank.

9) She helps Kirk and Spock, then decides to travel back with them to the 23rd century.

10) The charge for which Kirk is demoted from Admiral to Captain at the film's end.

➤ Star Trek V: The Final Frontier

1) Which member of the Star Trek cast directed this film?

2) What planet in the neutral zone is known as the "Planet of Galactic Peace"?

3) Name the capital city of this planet captured by the Vulcan Sybok and his gang.

4) What is the relationship between Spock and Sybok?

5) The location where Sybok believes God can be found.

6) What is the Vulcan name for the single planet believed to exist at the center of the galaxy?

7) Kirk, Spock, McCoy and Sybok take this shuttlecraft to explore the planet.

8) Who plays Sybok?

9) What does Kirk say to the energy being when questioning whether he is, as he claims, God?

10) Where do Kirk, Spock and McCoy go for shore leave after this adventure?

➤ *Star Trek VI: The Undiscovered Country*

1) What is Sulu's rank?

2) What disaster will render the Klingon's home planet uninhabitable within 50 years?

3) Name the Klingon emissary Kirk must escort to the peace summit.

4) Describe the sentence given by the Klingon court to Kirk and McCoy for the murder of the Klingon emissary.

5) What well-known actor plays General Chang?

6) Which Federation officers are part of the conspiracy to sabotage the peace talks?

7) Which cast member of *Star Trek: The Next Generation* plays Kirk and Spock's Klingon defense attorney?

8) From which play of Shakespeare's does the phrase "the undiscovered country" come from?

9) Where are the peace talks being held?

10) She was the shape-shifting Chameloid who helps Kirk and Spock escape from prison.

ANSWERS

➤ *Star Trek: The Motion Picture*

1) Willard Decker
2) Admiral
3) Kolinahr
4) He invokes a little-used reserve activation clause.
5) V'ger
6) Ilia, a Deltan female
7) It was the Voyager spacecraft transformed into an artificial intelligence of superior power by aliens on a machine planet
8) He uses the Vulcan mind meld
9) To communicate with its creator
10) Captain Decker

➤ *Star Trek II: The Wrath of Khan*

1) Kirstie Alley
2) Khan Noonian Singh
3) Ceti Alpha V
4) The Ceti Eel, which enters through the ear and burrows into the human brain
5) Dr. Carol Marcus, a codeveloper of the genesis project

6) U.S.S. Reliant

7) Project Genesis

8) His katra, or living spirit

9) The Mutara Nebula

10) David Marcus

➤ *Star Trek III: The Search for Spock*

1) To recover Spock's body so Spock's living spirit can be transferred to it from McCoy's mind

2) James B. Sikking

3) NX-2000

4) Transwarp drive

5) Christopher Lloyd

6) Maltz

7) Leonard Nimoy

8) T'Lar

9) fal-tor-pan

10) A Bird of Prey

➤ *Star Trek IV: The Voyage Home*

1) Leonard Nimoy

2) San Francisco, California, Earth

3) The Bounty

4) Humpback whales

5) A slingshot effect caused by whipping the ship around the sun

6) Golden Gate Park (a cloaking device keeps the ship invisible)

7) George and Gracie

8) Transparent aluminum

9) Dr. Gilliam Taylor

10) Disobeying the orders of a superior officer

➤ Star Trek V: The Final Frontier

1) William Shatner

2) Nimbus III

3) Paradise City

4) They are half brothers (Sybok is Sarek's son by a Vulcan priestess)

5) The Great Barrier at the center of the galaxy

6) Sha Ka Ree

7) Copernicus

8) Laurence Luckinbill

9) "Excuse me, excuse me. But what does God need with a starship?"

10) Yosemite National Park

➤ Star Trek VI: The Undiscovered Country

1) Captain of the U.S.S. Excelsior

2) The explosion of Praxis, the Klingon's key energy-producing facility

3) Chancellor Gorkon of the Klingon High Council

4) Life imprisonment with hard labor in the dilithium mines of the penal asteroid Rura Penthe

5) Christopher Plummer

6) Admiral Cartwright and Lieutenant Valeris

7) Michael Dorn

8) Hamlet

9) Khitomer

10) Martia

➤ *Gene Roddenberry: A Life I*

1) Name the *Star Trek* actress who became Gene Roddenberry's wife.

2) When and where was Gene Roddenberry born?

3) What did his father do for a living?

4) Where did Roddenberry attend college and what did he major in?

5) What nickname did *Star Trek* fans give Roddenberry?

6) What jobs did Gene Roddenberry hold before becoming a TV writer?

7) Where did Roddenberry almost lose his life in a plane crash?

8) What did Roddenberry do in World War II?

9) When did Roddenberry receive his star on Hollywood's walk of fame?

10) Whom did Roddenberry consider the "Alfred Hitchcock of science fiction"?

➤ *Writings*

1) Under what pen name did Roddenberry begin his literary career?

2) Roddenberry wrote the pilot episode for this science fiction television series starring Robert Foxworth as an android.

3) He also wrote the script for this 1971 MGM movie starring Rock Hudson.

4) How much money did Roddenberry charge for providing the plot for the *Star Trek* episode "Who Mourns for Adonis?", credited to Gilbert Ralston and Gene L. Coon?

5) Which of the following *Star Trek* episodes did Roddenberry write the script for?
   A) "The Menagerie"
   B) "Return to Tomorrow"
   C) "Bread and Circuses"
   D) "The Cage"
   E) "The Omega Glory"

6) In 1952 Gene Roddenberry sold a science fiction script for a show that featured *Wrath of Khan* star Ricardo Montalban. What was the title of the script?

7) Which of the following TV series did Gene Roddenberry write scripts for?

A) "Dr. Kildare"

B) "Highway Patrol"

C) "The Jane Wyman Show"

D) "The Naked City"

E) "The Kaiser Aluminum Hour"

F) "Dr. Christian"

8) What was Gene Roddenberry's first TV series?

9) For what TV series did Roddenberry serve as head writer?

10) With whom did Roddenberry coauthor the pilot episode for *Star Trek: The Next Generation?*

➤ *More Writings*

1) What periodical published poetry written by Gene Roddenberry?

2) With whom did Roddenberry coauthor a book celebrating the 25th anniversary of *Star Trek?*

3) What was the title of the science fiction novel Roddenberry started to write but never completed?

4) With whom did Roddenberry coauthor the theme to *Star Trek?*

5) Roddenberry wrote a 17-page script for a movie about this fictional character, a copy of which is on file in the Edgar Rice Burroughs Collection of the University of Louisville.

6) When did Gene Roddenberry sell his first TV script?

7) Name the title of the nonfiction book Roddenberry ghost-wrote for Los Angeles Police Chief William Parker.

8) What science fiction TV series did Roddenberry write following *Star Trek*?

9) This is the title of Roddenberry's unsold Screen Gems script about Sam Houston.

10) Which of these TV series did Roddenberry write for?
   A) "Mr. District Attorney"
   B) "The West Point Story"
   C) "Harbor Command"
   D) "Bat Masterson"
   E) "Boots and Saddles"
   F) "Jefferson Drum"

➤ *The Great Creator and Star Trek*

1) How much development money did NBC pay Roddenberry to write a pilot script for *Star Trek*?

2) Who was Roddenberry's choice for Spock in case Leonard Nimoy turned down the part?

3) Which episode of *Star Trek* was Roddenberry's favorite, and who wrote it?

4) What Gene Roddenberry story (unpro-

duced) for *Genesis II* became the basic plot for *Star Trek: The Motion Picture*?

5) What was Roddenberry's involvement in *Star Trek: The Next Generation*?

6) What was his role on *Star Trek: The Animated Series*, the Saturday morning Trek cartoon?

7) Who was Roddenberry's first choice for an actor to play Captain Kirk?

8) In which season of *Star Trek* was Roddenberry replaced as producer?

9) What beer featured Gene Roddenberry as a spokesperson in its magazine advertisements?

10) What motivated Roddenberry to produce a spoken-word *Star Trek* record album featuring the cast of the show?

➤ *Gene Roddenberry: A Life II*

1) Who was Roddenberry's first wife?

2) Where did Roddenberry learn to fly?

3) Where did Roddenberry study poetry and short story writing?

4) What was the name of the airplane Roddenberry was piloting when he crashed in the desert?

5) To what unit was Roddenberry assigned while in the Army?

6) Where did Roddenberry nearly have a second plane crash when the controls on his aircraft froze?

7) What police group was Roddenberry a spokesperson for?

8) What TV pilot did Roddenberry write based on his experience as a police officer?

9) What Roddenberry series (never produced) was set underwater in the year 2115?

10) When and how did Gene Roddenberry die?

ANSWERS

➤ *Gene Roddenberry: A Life I*

1) Majel Barrett (Nurse Chapel)
2) August 19, 1921, in El Paso, Texas
3) He was a police officer
4) L.A. City College and then U.C.L.A., where he majored in engineering
5) The Great Bird of the Galaxy
6) Airline pilot for Pan Am and a Los Angeles police officer
7) In the Syrian desert, during a flight out of Calcutta
8) He was a reconnaissance pilot at Guadalcanal
9) September 4, 1985
10) Science fiction writer Isaac Asimov

➤ *Writings*

1) Robert Wesley (his brother's first name combined with his middle name)
2) "The Questor Tapes"
3) *Pretty Maids All in a Row*
4) $750
5) A, B, C, D, E

6) "The Secret Defense of 117"

7) A, B, C, D, E, F

8) "The Lieutenant"

9) "Have Gun—Will Travel"

10) D.C. Fontana

➤ *More Writings*

1) *The New York Times*

2) Susan Sackett (the book was never published)

3) *Report from Earth*

4) Alexander Courage wrote the music;
Roddenberry, the lyrics

5) Tarzan of the Apes

6) 1951

7) *Parker on Police*

8) "Genesis II"

9) "The Man from Texas"

10) A, B, C, D, E, F

➤ *The Great Creator and Star Trek*

1) $20,000

2) Martin Landau

3) "The City on the Edge of Forever," by
Harlan Ellison

4) "Robot's Return"

5) He was the executive producer

6) He was the executive consultant

7) Lloyd Bridges

8) In the second season

9) Guinness

10) It would provide a convenient way to answer fans' questions about the show

➤ *Gene Roddenberry: A Life II*

1) Eileen Anita Rexroat

2) The Army Civilian Pilot Training program

3) Columbia University

4) Pan Am Clipper Eclipse

5) 394th squadron, 5th bombardment group

6) LaGuardia Field

7) The Association for Professional Law Enforcement

8) "Tribunes," a futuristic cop show

9) "Magna"

10) He died of a heart attack on October 24, 1991

➤ Authors I

Match the screenwriter in the numbered list with the *Star Trek* episode he or she wrote in the lettered list.

1) Carey Wilbur
2) Robert Hamner
3) Art Wallace
4) Margaret Armen
5) Meyer Dolinsky
6) Jerome Bixby
7) Lee Erwin
8) David Gerrold
9) Jean Lisette Aroestei
10) Arthur H. Singer

A) "Turnabout Intruder"
B) "All Our Yesterdays"
C) "The Trouble with Tribbles"
D) "Whom Gods Destroy"

E) "The Day of the Dove"

F) "Plato's Stepchildren"

G) "The Paradise Syndrome"

H) "Assignment: Earth"

I) "A Taste of Armageddon"

J) "Space Seed"

➤ Authors II

Match the screenwriter in the numbered list with the *Star Trek* episode he or she wrote in the lettered list.

1) D.C. Fontana

2) Gilbert A. Ralston

3) Gene L. Coon

4) Boris Sobelman

5) Don Ingalls

6) Paul Schneider

7) John D. Black

8) Jerry Sohl

9) Stephen W. Carabatsos

10) John Meredyth Lucas

A) "Friday's Child"

B) "Who Mourns for Adonis?"

C) "The Devil in the Dark"

D) "The Return of the Archons"

E) "The Alternative Factor"

F) "Balance of Terror"

G) "The Naked Time"

H) "The Corbomite Maneuver"

I) "Operation: Annihilate!"

J) "The Changeling"

➤ *Celebrity Trek Writers*

1) This star of the children's TV show *Lamb Chop's Play-Along* coauthored the *Star Trek* episode "The Lights of Zetar," with Jeremy Tarcher.

2) Author of the highly acclaimed *Star Trek* episode "The City on the Edge of Forever," he is the author of many classic science fiction stories including "I Have No Mouth and I Must Scream."

3) This *Psycho* author wrote the *Star Trek* episode "Catspaw" in which an alien witch turns into a giant black cat.

4) This well-known science fiction author, who wrote the *Star Trek* episode "Shore Leave," also wrote *The Dreaming Jewels,* a science fiction novel featuring an ant-eating boy named Hortie.

5) The *Star Trek* episode "The Doomsday Machine" was written by this famous "new wave" science fiction author.

6) Which science fiction writer and author of more than 400 books was a special consultant to the movie *Star Trek: The Motion Picture*?

7) In addition to coauthoring the script for *Star Trek IV*, he wrote the critically acclaimed Sherlock Holmes novel *The Seven Percent Solution*.

8) A published poet, he contributed to the script of *Star Trek IV*.

9) What "hard science fiction" writer, author of *Ringworld,* wrote the *Star Trek* episode "The Slave Weapon"?

10) What science fiction novelist co-wrote the script of *Star Trek V*?

ANSWERS

➤ *Authors I*

1) J
2) I
3) H
4) G
5) F
6) E
7) D
8) C
9) B
10) A

➤ *Authors II*

1) A
2) B
3) C
4) D
5) E
6) F
7) G
8) H
9) I
10) J

➤ *Celebrity Trek Writers*

1) Shari Lewis
2) Harlan Ellison
3) Robert Bloch
4) Theodore Sturgeon
5) Norman Spinrad
6) Isaac Asimov
7) Nicholas Meyer
8) Leonard Nimoy
9) Larry Niven
10) William Shatner

➤ Novels and Authors I

Match the *Star Trek* novel in the numbered list with the name of its author in the lettered list.

1) *Strangers from the Sky*
2) *Final Frontier*
3) *The Wounded Sky*
4) *My Enemy, My Ally*
5) *The Starless World*
6) *Enterprise: The First Adventure*
7) *Shell Game*
8) *Devil World*
9) *Spock Must Die*
10) *Messiah!*

A) Diane Carey
B) Vonda McIntyre
C) Harlan Ellison
D) Rob Kaplan

E) Diane Duane

F) Theodore R. Cogswell

G) James Blish

H) Margaret Wander Bonnano

I) Melissa Crandall

J) Gordon Eklund

➤ *Novels and Authors II*

Match the *Star Trek* novel in the numbered list with its author in the lettered list.

1) *Star Trek: The Motion Picture*

2) *The Entropy Effect*

3) *The Klingon Gambit*

4) *Corona*

5) *Shadow Lord*

6) *Mindshadow*

7) *Encounter at Farpoint*

8) *Ice Trap*

9) *The Starship Trap*

10) *Final Frontier*

A) Greg Bear

B) J.M. Dillard

C) Gene Roddenberry

D) Mel Gilden

E) Diane Cary

F) David Gerrold

G) L.A. Graf

H) Vonda N. McIntyre

I) Laurence Yep

J) Robert W. Vardeman

➤ Novels and Authors III

Match the *Star Trek* novel in the numbered list with its author in the lettered list.

1) *Vendetta*

2) *Strangers from the Sky*

3) *Metamorphosis*

4) *The Final Nexus*

5) *The Starless World*

6) *Planet of Judgment*

7) *The Abode of Life*

8) *Yesterday's Son*

9) *The Vulcan Academy Murders*

10) *Timetrap*

A) Peter David

B) Margaret Bonanno

C) Jean Lorrah

D) Gene deWeese

E) Gordon Eklund

F) Joe Haldeman

G) Lee Correy

H) Ann Crispin

I) Joan Lorrah

J) David Dvorkin

➤ *Novel Plots I*

Match the *Star Trek* novel in the numbered list with its plot in the lettered list.

1) *Spock Must Die!*

2) *Spock Messiah!*

3) *World Without End*

4) *Perry's Planet*

5) *Doctor's Orders*

6) *Home is the Hunter*

7) *Vulcan's Glory*

8) *The Kobayashi Maru*

9) *Dreams of the Raven*

10) *Vulcan!*

A) The Enterprise passes through an energy-draining magnetic field

B) Kirk puts McCoy in charge of the Enterprise

C) Spock searches for a rare Vulcan stone

D) Sulu goes back in time to medieval Japan

E) Spock is duplicated in a transporter accident

F) The Enterprise crew visits a planet where a

virus causes people to collapse when they get violent

G) Brain-sucking beings swallow consciousness of Starfleet personnel

H) Biologist Dr. Ktalya Tremain is prejudiced against Vulcans

I) Kirk's shuttlecraft is hit by a gravitic mine

J) Spock's mind is tampered with and he tries to take over a planet

➤ Novel Plots II

Match the *Star Trek* novel in the numbered list with its plot in the lettered list.

1) *The Entropy Effect*
2) *The Prometheus Design*
3) *The Abode of Life*
4) *Blackfire*
5) *Triangle*
6) *Yesterday's Son*
7) *Mutiny on the Enterprise*
8) *The Wounded Sky*
9) *Corona*
10) *My Enemy, My Ally*

A) Romulans gain telepathic powers

B) Vulcan children fall under the influence of a being preparing to wipe out the universe

C) The Enterprise crew builds a new universe using the best qualities drawn from each person

D) The crew of the Enterprise, under mind control, mutinies

E) Spock has a son

F) The Oneness and Totality force individuals to bond with them

G) An explosion aboard the Enterprise seriously injures Kirk, Spock, Uhura and Chekhov

H) A gravity disturbance hurls the Enterprise to a planet in the Sagittarius arm

I) A crisis on planet Helvan

J) Kirk dies

➤ Novel Plots III

Match the *Star Trek* novel in the numbered list with its plot in the lettered list.

1) *The Vulcan Academy Murders*

2) *Killing Time*

3) *Dwellers in the Crucible*

4) *Battlestations*

5) *The Three-Minute Universe*

6) *Ghost Walker*

7) *Faces of Fire*

8) *The Disinherited*

9) *Ice Trap*

10) *Sanctuary*

A) Kirk buys a sailboat

B) Kirk's body is taken over by an alien

C) A starship is run by murderous children

D) Kirk's son and Spock attempt to foil a Klingon plot

E) Spock's mother is under a death threat from an unknown killer

F) Uhura is assigned to another starship

G) The Enterprise chases a pirate ship

H) The Enterprise crew is trapped on an ice-covered planet

I) Romulans disrupt time

J) A women's prison story

➤ *Fan Fiction*

1) What is a "K/S" story?

2) What is a fanzine?

3) What is a "Mary Sue" story?

4) Name Spock's son by a Vulcan ambassador.

5) What is the official name of the Uhura fan club?

6) Name the fanzine dedicated to Chekhov.

7) What is the official name of Lieutenant William Riker's fan club?

8) What is the official name of the Chekhov fan club?

9) What is the title of a fan novel combining *Star Trek* with "The Man from U.N.C.L.E."?

10) What is the title of the fanzine dedicated to Dr. McCoy?

11) What is the title of the newsletter on Brent Spiner?

12) What is the title of the Leonard Nimoy fanzine?

ANSWERS

➤ Novels and Authors I

1) H
2) A
3) E
4) E
5) J
6) B
7) I
8) J
9) G
10) F

➤ Novels and Authors II

1) C
2) H
3) J
4) A
5) I
6) B
7) F
8) G
9) D
10) E

➤ Novels and Authors III

1) A
2) B
3) C
4) D
5) E
6) F
7) G
8) H
9) I
10) J

➤ Novel Plots I

1) E
2) J
3) A
4) F
5) B
6) D
7) C
8) I
9) G
10) H

➤ Novel Plots II

1) J
2) I
3) H
4) G
5) F
6) E
7) D
8) C
9) B
10) A

➤ Novel Plots III

1) E
2) I
3) J
4) A
5) C
6) B
7) D
8) F
9) H
10) G

➤ *Fan Fiction*

1) A fan story (*Star Trek* story written by an amateur) in which Kirk and Spock become lovers

2) An amateur publication about *Star Trek*, produced by a fan, with a typical print run of from 10 to 1,000 copies

3) A fan story in which a young girl, usually from the 20th century, who is pretty, intelligent and a loner, comes to be aboard the Enterprise

4) Sahaj

5) Friends of Nichelle Nichols

6) A Russian Inwention/Security Check

7) Fans and Followers of Jonathan Frakes

8) Walter Koenig International

9) Future Tense Affair

10) Dr. McCoy's Medical Log

11) Data Entries

12) Contrast

➤ *Saturday Mornings in Outer Space I*

1) Who was the associate producer for the *Star Trek* animated series?

2) Who served as executive consultant?

3) What company produced the cartoon?

4) What *Star Trek* cast member wrote scripts for the series?

5) Who produced the special effects?

6) When did the first episode air?

7) A giant clone of which scientist almost kills Spock by cloning him?

8) Name an animal that eats tribbles.

9) What is the Vulcan coming-of-age ceremony called?

10) What was the name of the pet sehlat Spock had as a boy?

11) What award did the *Star Trek* animated series win?

12) Which cast members from the original *Star Trek* TV show returned to do voices for the characters in the animated series?

➤ *Saturday Mornings in Outer Space II*

1) Name the race of alien, golden-skinned women who survived by draining the life force from kidnapped males.

2) What was the name of the devil-like creature the Enterprise crew encounters in the magic dimension?

3) What is the name of the region of space where many ships have disappeared—the outer space equivalent of the Bermuda Triangle?

4) What is a stasis box?

5) What was the first race to venture into outer space?

6) Name the underwater inhabitants of the water planet Argo.

7) What world was populated by miniature people who were mutated human beings from Earth?

8) On what planet is the dominant life form an intelligent slug?

9) What planet is McCoy accused of causing a plague on?

10) What is the only known antidote to the disease choriocytosis, which causes suffocation in Vulcans after three days?

ANSWERS

➤ *Saturday Mornings in Outer Space I*

1) D.C. Fontana

2) Gene Roddenberry

3) Filmation Associates

4) Walter Koenig

5) Reuben Timmins

6) September 1973

7) Dr. Starros Keniclius

8) A glommer

9) Kahs-wan

10) I-Chaya

11) It won an Emmy for Best Children's Series for the 1974-1975 TV season

12) William Shatner, Leonard Nimoy, DeForest Kelley, George Takei, Nichelle Nichols, Majel Barrett, James Doohan

➤ *Saturday Mornings in Outer Space II*

1) The Taureans

2) Lucien

3) The Delta Triangle

4) The last remnant of the Slaver civilization, a long-dead race that once ruled the galaxy

5) The Vedala

6) Aquans

7) Terra Ten

8) Lactra

9) Dramia II

10) Strobolin

➤ *Aliens I*

1) This race produced supersoldiers using biochemical and psychological manipulation.

    A) Romulans
    B) Angosians
    C) Klingons
    D) Talosians
    E) Vulcans

2) They kidnapped Jean Luc Picard.

    A) Ferengi
    B) Betazoids
    C) Borg
    D) Archons
    E) Organians

3) What race used their superhuman powers to prevent all-out war between the Federation and the Klingons?

    A) Vulcans
    B) Vegans

C) Talosians
D) Organians
E) Hobokenites

4) Of what race is Ensign Ro of the Enterprise?
   A) Bajoran
   B) Cardassian
   C) Solarion
   D) Tamarian
   E) Morphazoid

5) The leader of this race was named after Kirk and McCoy.
   A) Archans
   B) Karidians
   C) Zibalians
   D) Zalkonians
   E) Capellans

6) Soren, a pilot of this race, is found guilty by her people of having a forbidden love affair with William Riker.
   A) J'naii
   B) Trill
   C) Turkanians
   D) Benzites
   E) Allasmorphs

7) What race must carry their native atmosphere, for breathing purposes, in a dish located below their mouth and nose?
   A) Koinonians
   B) Benzites
   C) Husnock

D) Mintakans
E) Barzans

8) Name the race, at the Bronze Age of evolution, that resembles primitive Vulcans.

   A) Husnock
   B) Barzans
   C) Mintakans
   D) Ansata
   E) Zibalians

9) Criminals from this alien race attempt to steal a weapon that can destroy stars.

   A) Kelvans
   B) Vorgons
   C) Kataans
   D) Borg
   E) Kriosians

10) They kidnapped Captain Christopher Pike.

   A) Talosians
   B) Organians
   C) Kalandans
   D) Sumarians
   E) Ardanians

➤ Aliens II

1) From what race was the giant lizard star-ship captain whom Kirk battled?

   A) Q
   B) Ongrans

C) Lizarians
D) Gorn
E) Iotians

2) What type of creature is native to Daled IV?

A) Morphazoid
B) Changeling
C) Hermaphrodite
D) Polymorph
E) Allasmorph

3) This race kidnaps Geordi LaForge in an attempt to steal Federation weapons technology.

A) Antedan
B) Kriosian
C) Kataan
D) Pakled
E) Romulan

4) This race steals Spock's brain.

A) Cherons
B) Melkots
C) Talosians
D) Thulians
E) Eymorgs

5) Which race has pointy ears similar to Vulcans?

A) Mermen
B) Romulans
C) Klingons
D) Transonians
E) Capellans

6) What advanced alien race gave Charlie X his powers?
   A) Thasians
   B) Krill
   C) Skree
   D) Cappellans
   E) Q

7) They attempted to trap the Enterprise in an energy web generated by their starships.
   A) Thasians
   B) Bajorans
   C) Tholians
   D) Cardassians
   E) Klingons

8) Data is a(n):
   A) robot
   B) cyborg
   C) android
   D) bionic man
   E) clone

9) Who tortured Picard?
   A) Romulans
   B) Ferengi
   C) Hood
   D) Cardassians
   E) Borg

10) Gary Seven, the time traveler Kirk and Spock meet on Earth in 1968, is:

A) Martian
B) Human
C) Venusian
D) Thalosian
E) None of the above

ANSWERS

➤ *Aliens I*

1) B
2) C
3) D
4) A
5) E
6) A
7) B
8) C
9) B
10) A

➤ *Aliens II*

1) D
2) E
3) D
4) E
5) B
6) A
7) C
8) C
9) D
10) B

➤ *Gods and Semi-Gods I*

1) In which *Star Trek* movie does the Enterprise travel to the center of the galaxy in search of God?

2) This superbeing calls himself the "Squire of Gothos."

3) This godlike being, who held the Enterprise and its crew captive on planet Pollux IV, was immortal and had an extra organ in his body that enabled him to absorb and use external sources of energy.

4) By absorbing the element kironide into their thyroid glands, this race gained tremendous mental powers, including telekinesis, the ability to move objects using their minds.

5) These disembodied, powerful creatures live on a world located on the boundary of Federation space and the Klingon empire.

6) He gained superhuman powers when the Enterprise encountered an energy barrier at the edge of the galaxy.

7) What powerful entity, posing as human Kevin Uxbridge, destroyed an entire race in an act of revenge?

8) He is Picard's sometime-foe and one of the most powerful beings in the universe.

9) What race of ultrapowerful beings forces Kirk to fight a starship captain of another race to the death?

10) This genetically engineered superman once ruled more than a quarter of Earth.

➤ Gods and Semi-Gods II

1) What seemingly powerful alien being who holds the Enterprise captive turns out to be a puppet manipulated by a child-like alien?

2) When this teenager with superpowers becomes angry with Spock, he uses his mental powers to break Spock's legs.

3) Name the machine-God of the planet Gamma Trianguli VI.

4) How old is the Guardian of Forever?

5) Name the superpowerful, self-aware space probe that destroyed the Malurian System and thought Captain Kirk was its creator.

6) What device does the Spock of a parallel universe use to take control of that universe?

7) These powerful creatures, which abduct Kirk, Uhura and Chekhov using a long-distance transporter beam, are brains contained within a glass dome.

8) What powerful beings create a replica of the O.K. Corral to test Kirk and his landing party?

9) Name the evil entity who controls people's minds and takes over the Enterprise with the intent of traveling to other planets where he can corrupt the innocent.

10) The natives of this planet, gifted with tremendous physical and energy powers, are half-black and half-white.

ANSWERS

➤ *Gods and Semi-Gods I*

1) *Star Trek V: The Final Frontier*
2) Trelane
3) Apollo
4) Platonians
5) Organians
6) Gary Mitchell
7) The Douwd
8) Q
9) Metrons
10) Khan

➤ *Gods and Semi-Gods II*

1) Balok
2) Charlie X
3) Vaal
4) More than 5 billion years old
5) Nomad
6) The Tantalus Field
7) The Providers
8) Melkots
9) Gorgan
10) Cheron

➤ *Planets I*

Match the planet in the numbered list with its description in the lettered list.

1) Ekos
2) 829-IV
3) Earth
4) Elba II
5) Ardana
6) Skorr
7) Yolanda
8) Pandro
9) Gothos
10) Genesis

A) A gladiator planet with 20th century Earth technology
B) The Cloud City of Strathos is located here
C) Home to a race of birdpeople
D) The twin of the planet Zeos
E) The natives can split themselves into three separate beings

F) A mental asylum

G) Located in Quadrant 904

H) Artificially created world made of pro-
tomatter

I) A hollowed-out asteroid

J) Location of Starfleet headquarters

➤ *Planets II*

Match the planet in the numbered list with its
description in the lettered list.

1) Kelva

2) L-370

3) Ceti Alpha V

4) Gamma Hydra IV

5) Halcon

6) Levinius V

7) Rigel II

8) Gamma Canaris

9) Janov IV

10) Mantilles

A) Destroyed by a doomsday machine

B) The natives are shape-changers

C) Everyone who visits there dies of acceler-
ated aging

D) Population was wiped out by mind para-
sites

E) A planetary vacation resort

F) Kirk marooned Khan here

G) The Horta's home

H) Earth colony run by Governor Bob Wesley

I) Zefram Cochrane lives here

J) A planet ravaged by magnetic storms

➤ *Planets III*

Match the planet in the numbered list with its description in the lettered list.

1) Christopher Pike and his crew were attacked by a warrior tribe on which planet?

2) Name the planet on which Spock is reborn.

3) When Kirk beams up from this planet, he splits into two Kirks, one good and one bad.

4) On this planet, fruits and plants are filled with poison and acid.

5) What planet was colonized by the nanites, a race of tiny beings newly evolved from robots?

6) Q uses his powers to save this planet from destruction by restoring the orbit of its moon.

7) Natives of this planet communicate using a unique language based on metaphors from their mythology.

8) On what planet does Riker meet Etana?

9) the mythical planet at the center of the galaxy.

10) The Enterprise-C, under the command of Captain Rachel Garrett, is nearly destroyed defending this planet from Romulan attack.

➤ *Planets IV*

1) What planet is Deanna Troi from?

2) On what colony was Tasha Yar held prisoner?

3) The powerful she-devil Ardra claims this planet's inhabitants sold themselves to her in exchange for a millennium of peace.

4) On which planet was Riker injured in a riot and hospitalized?

5) Name the planet endangered by a possible collision with a stellar core fragment being tracked by the Enterprise.

6) On this mining planet, a plasma fountain is used to transport materials from the surface to an orbiting space station.

7) Where did Kevin and Rishon Uxbridge live?

8) This planet is in orbit around a wormhole.

9) What is the home world of the nomadic Gatherers?

10) This planet is a gigantic arsenal selling advanced space weaponry to anyone who will pay the inhabitants' price.

ANSWERS

➤ *Planets I*

1) D
2) A
3) J
4) F
5) B
6) C
7) I
8) E
9) G
10) H

➤ *Planets II*

1) B
2) A
3) F
4) C
5) J
6) D
7) E
8) I
9) G
10) H

➤ *Planets III*

1) Rigel VII
2) Genesis
3) Alpha 177
4) Eden
5) Alpha IV
6) Bre'el IV
7) Tama
8) Risa
9) Shaka-Ree
10) Noarenda III

➤ *Planets IV*

1) Betazed
2) Turkana IV
3) Ventax II
4) Malcoria III
5) Moab IV
6) Tyrus VII
7) Rana IV
8) Barzan II
9) Acamar III
10) Minos

➤ High-Tech Trek I

1) It creates computer-simulated 3D artificial realities for recreational purposes aboard the Enterprise.

2) What is Kirk and Spock's favorite board game?

3) Where are dilithium crystals processed?

4) What device blanks out people's thought processes using pulsing lights and sounds?

5) This device renders Klingon ships invisible.

6) What hand-held Klingon weapon causes pain or kills by affecting the nervous system?

7) It is used to avoid nitrogen narcosis (the "bends") in crew members working in various pressures.

8) What type of propulsion system is faster than warp drive?

9) What are the hollowed-out asteroids from which the Federation watches the Neutral Zone called?

10) How fast is warp factor 3?

➤ *High-Tech Trek II*

1) Which alien race has perfected a mind control device?

2) What is the science of reshaping a planet's surface and atmosphere called?

3) What type of spacecraft was found to contain the frozen preserved remains of people from 20th century Earth?

4) How do impulse engines work?

5) What type of propulsion system is used aboard shuttlecraft?

6) What type of propulsion system is used aboard Enterprise lifeboats?

7) What is FWG-1?

8) At what speed do transwarp subspace communications travel?

9) What is done with leftover food and garbage from meals aboard the Enterprise?

10) What weapon did Kirk use to destroy the cloud creature of Tycho IV?

ANSWERS

➤ High-Tech Trek I

1) Holodeck
2) Tri-level chess
3) They are processed in "cracking plants"
4) Neural neutralizer
5) Cloaking device
6) Disrupter
7) Decompression chamber
8) Transwarp drive
9) Outposts
10) 27 times the speed of light

High-Tech Trek II

1) Ferengi
2) Terraforming
3) Cryosatellite
4) Impulse deflector crystal channels thrust energy from the vertical intermix chamber into the impulse unit
5) Ion propulsion or magnetic field drive
6) Particle-beam units
7) It refers to the nacelles containing the warp engines
8) 300 times the speed of light
9) It is resynthesized
10) Antimatter bomb

BIBLIOGRAPHY

Alexander, David. *Star Trek Creator: The Authorized Biography of Gene Roddenberry.* New York: ROC Books, 1994.

Asherman, Allan. *The Star Trek Compendium.* New York: Pocket Books, 1993.

Asherman, Allan. *The Star Trek Interview Book.* New York: Pocket Books, 1988.

Farrand, Phil. *The Nitpicker's Guide for Next Generation Trekkers.* New York: Dell, 1993.

Johnson, Shane. *Star Trek: Mr. Scott's Guide to the Enterprise.* New York: Pocket Books, 1987.

Nemecek, Larry. *The Star Trek: The Next Generation Companion.* New York: Pocket Books, 1992.

Okuda, Michael, and Okuda, Denise, *Star Trek Chronology: The History of the Future.* New York: Pocket Books, 1993.

Peel, John. *The Trek Encyclopedia: Second Edition.* Las Vegas: Pioneer, 1993.

Shatner, William, and Kreski, Chris. *Star Trek Memories.* New York: HarperCollins, 1993.

Takei, George. *To the Stars: The Autobiography of George Takei*. New York: Pocket Books, 1994.

Van Hise, James. *The Best of Enterprise Incidents: The Magazine for Star Trek Fans*. Las Vegas: Pioneer Books.

Van Hise, James. *The Classic Trek Crew Book*. Las Vegas: Pioneer Books, 1993.

Van Hise, James. *The Man Who Created Star Trek: Gene Roddenberry*. Las Vegas: Pioneer Books, 1992.

Van Hise, James. *The Special Effects of Star Trek*. Las Vegas: Pioneer Books, 1993.

Van Hise, James. *Trek: The Next Generation Crew Book*. Las Vegas: Pioneer Books, 1993.

Van Hise, James. *Trek Vs. The Next Generation*. Las Vegas: Pioneer Books, 1993.

Van Hise, James. *Trek: The Painted Adventure*. Las Vegas: Pioneer Books, 1993.

Van Hise, James. *The Voyage Continues. . . Trek: Deep Space Nine: The Unauthorized Story*. Las Vegas: Pioneer Books, 1993.

Van Hise, James. *The Voyage Continues. . . Trek: The Next Generation*, Second Edition. Las Vegas: Pioneer Books, 1992.

ABOUT THE AUTHOR

Robert W. Bly has been a science fiction and comic book fan for more than 30 years. He is the author of 27 books including *Creative Careers: Real Jobs in Glamour Fields* and *Secrets of a Freelance Writer*. His articles have appeared in such publications as *Writer's Digest, Amtrak Express, Cosmopolitan,* and *New Jersey Monthly.*

A chemical engineer by training, Mr. Bly is a full-time freelance writer working for such clients as IBM, AT&T, AlliedSignal, CoreStates Financial Corporation, Swiss Bank and EBI Medical Systems. He lives in New Milford, New Jersey, with his wife Amy and sons Alex and Stephen.